Above the Flood: Elevating Your Floodprone House

FEMA 347 / May 2000

FEMA

Acknowledgments

The support and contributions of the following individuals and organizations helped make the preparation of this publication possible:

James L. Witt
Director
Federal Emergency Management Agency

Michael J. Armstrong
Associate Director for Mitigation
Federal Emergency Management Agency

John Copenhaver
Regional Director
FEMA Region IV
Atlanta, Georgia

Clifford Oliver, CEM
Chief
Program Policy and Assessment Branch
Mitigation Directorate
Federal Emergency Management Agency

Paul Tertell, P.E.
Senior Engineer and Project Officer
Program Policy and Assessment Branch
Mitigation Directorate
Federal Emergency Management Agency

The Staff of the Mitigation Division
FEMA Region IV
Atlanta, Georgia

Cover photograph provided by **The Weather Channel.**

Table of Contents

CHAPTER 1

Introduction

Hurricane Andrew damaged hundreds of homes in south Florida.

In the early morning hours of August 24, 1992, Hurricane Andrew struck south Florida with high winds and heavy rains (Figure 1). Andrew destroyed tens of thousands of homes (Figure 2) and left 180,000 people homeless. The resulting property damage totaled over 30 billion dollars.

Figure 1
Hurricane Andrew was a Category 4 hurricane with peak winds of over 140 mph.

WARNING

The house elevation techniques described in this publication are appropriate only for houses **not** subject to the severe coastal flood hazards associated with high-velocity wave action from storms or seismic sources. See pages 2-2 through 2-4 for more information.

Figure 2
Damage to houses
and other buildings
was severe.

The widespread destruction caused by Andrew was due primarily to high
winds (Figure 3). However, flood waters contributed to the damage in low-
lying coastal areas of central and southern Miami-Dade County (Figure 4).

Figure 3
Wind damage.

Figure 4
In low-lying areas, wind and rain damage to interior finishes and furnishings was exacerbated by flood waters.

DEFINITION

In a **slab-on-grade** house, the floor of the house is formed by a concrete slab that sits directly on the ground.

In the repair and reconstruction efforts that followed Hurricane Andrew, owners of damaged houses had opportunities to modify their houses to protect them from future flood damage. One effective method of protecting a house from flooding is elevating the habitable areas of the house above the flood level.

Almost all single-family homes in Miami-Dade County are constructed with reinforced masonry block walls on a **slab-on-grade** foundation. Houses of this type are the most difficult to elevate for flood protection. This publication describes how homeowners in Miami-Dade County elevated their damaged slab-on-grade masonry houses following the devastating effects of Hurricane Andrew.

DEFINITION

The **Federal Emergency Management Agency (FEMA)** is the independent Federal agency that administers the National Flood Insurance Program (NFIP).

Chapter 2 of this publication explains how the **Federal Emergency Management Agency (FEMA)** provided technical and regulatory guidance to Miami-Dade County homeowners concerning alternative house elevation techniques. Chapter 3 presents an overview of three common techniques appropriate for a variety of houses on different types of foundations. Chapter 4 uses eight illustrated case studies to demonstrate how Miami-Dade County homeowners used the three techniques to elevate their slab-on-grade houses. The benefits of elevating a floodprone house are summarized in Chapter 5.

For information about obtaining videotape and CD-ROM versions of this publication, refer to Chapter 6.

Homeowner Options

FEMA provided on-site guidance to homeowners concerning repair options compliant with the local floodplain management ordinance.

National Flood Insurance Program

The repair of damaged houses in floodprone areas of Miami-Dade County is governed by floodplain management regulations enacted by the county as a participant in the National Flood Insurance Program (NFIP). The

National Flood Insurance Program

NFIP

Administered by FEMA

NFIP is a Federal program that helps communities reduce flood risks and enables property owners and renters to buy flood insurance. The program is administered by FEMA.

Communities participate in the NFIP by enacting and enforcing floodplain management regulations to reduce future flood risks. At a minimum, these regulations govern construction in the **Special Flood Hazard Areas (SFHAs)** shown on Flood Insurance Rate Maps (FIRMs) issued by FEMA (Figure 5).

DEFINITION

The **Special Flood Hazard Area (SFHA)** is the area inundated by the flood that has a 1-percent probability of being equaled or exceeded during any given year. The NFIP regulations refer to this flood as the "base flood."

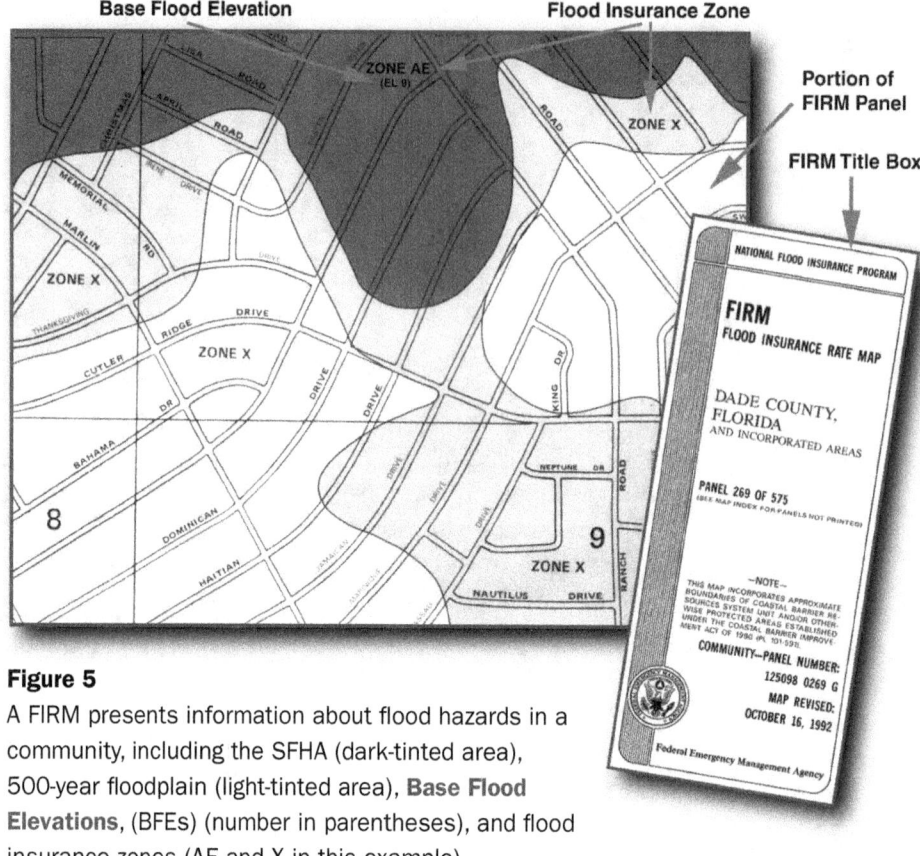

Figure 5
A FIRM presents information about flood hazards in a community, including the SFHA (dark-tinted area), 500-year floodplain (light-tinted area), **Base Flood Elevations**, (BFEs) (number in parentheses), and flood insurance zones (AE and X in this example).

DEFINITION

The **Base Flood Elevation (BFE)** is the elevation of the flood that has a 1-percent probability of being equaled or exceeded in any given year. The NFIP regulations refer to this flood as the "base flood."

Note that the SFHA in the example in Figure 5 is designated Zone AE. This zone is only one of several applied to SFHAs under the NFIP, including V, VE, V1-V30, A, AE, A1-A30, AO, and AH. These zones indicate differences in the types and severity of flood hazards in SFHAs. For the purposes of this publication, it is sufficient to focus on the basic differences between the two main types of SFHA zones—V zones and A zones. The distinction is important because regulatory requirements associated with V zones and A zones differ significantly. As explained later in this chapter, these requirements affect the types of building elevation techniques that may be used under the NFIP.

V zones (VE, V1-V30, and V) identify Coastal High Hazard Areas, which are SFHAs subject to high-velocity wave action from storms or seismic sources. The hazards in V zones include not only inundation by flood waters, but also the impact of waves and waterborne debris and the effects of severe scour and erosion. In contrast, A zones identify SFHAs not within the Coastal High Hazard Area. Although A zones and V zones both identify areas at risk from the base flood, the severity of the flood hazard is less in A zones, primarily because high-velocity wave action either is not present or is less significant than in V zones. Consequently, wave and debris impact, erosion, and scour hazards are less severe in A zones.

A participating community must regulate three types of building construction in the SFHA (in both V zones and A zones):

- new construction
- substantial improvements to existing buildings
- repairs of substantially damaged buildings

For floodplain management purposes, the NFIP regulations, at Section 59.1 of the U.S. Code of Federal Regulations (CFR), define new construction, substantial improvement, and substantial damage as follows:

- **New construction** – structures for which the start of construction commenced on or after the effective date of a floodplain management regulation adopted by a community and includes any subsequent improvements to such structures.

- **Substantial improvement** – any reconstruction, rehabilitation, addition, or other improvement of a structure, the cost of which equals or exceeds 50 percent of the market value of the structure before the start of construction of the improvement.

- **Substantial damage** – damage of any origin sustained by a structure whereby the cost of restoring the structure to its before damaged condition would equal or exceed 50 percent of the market value of the structure before the damage occurred.

If a building is significantly damaged by **any** cause, not just by flooding, the community's floodplain administrator—who may or may not be the local building official—must determine whether the building is *substantially damaged*, as defined above. FEMA does not play a direct role in this determination. Rather, FEMA's role and that of the NFIP State Coordinator is to provide technical assistance to local officials who administer community ordinances that meet the NFIP minimum floodplain management requirements.

Each participating community must require that new residential buildings, substantially improved residential buildings, and substantially damaged residential buildings be elevated above the BFE so that the potential for future flood damage is reduced. The elevation techniques that may be used under the NFIP depend on whether the building to be elevated is in a V zone or an A zone.

In a V zone, the NFIP regulations require that the building be elevated on an open foundation (e.g., pilings, posts, piers) and that the bottom of the **lowest horizontal structural member** (e.g., floor support beam) be at or above the BFE. In other words, a building in a V zone may not be supported by continuous walls below the BFE. The basis for this requirement is that continuous walls, and therefore the building they support, are more susceptible to damage from the additional hazards present in V zones—wave impact, waterborne debris impact, scour, and erosion, as discussed previously.

DEFINITION

Under the NFIP regulations, the **lowest floor** of a house or other building is the lowest floor of the lowest enclosed area, *including a basement.*

In A zones, where flood hazards are less severe, buildings may be elevated either on an open foundation or on continuous foundation walls below the BFE (Figure 6). Regardless of the type of foundation used, A-zone buildings must be elevated so that the **lowest floor** is at or above the BFE, as shown in Figure 6. If continuous walls are used below the BFE, they must be equipped with openings that allow flood waters to flow into and out of the area enclosed by the walls (Figure 6). Allowing the entry and exit of flood waters ensures that water pressures will be the same on both sides of the walls and reduces the likelihood that water pressure will cause the walls to fail.

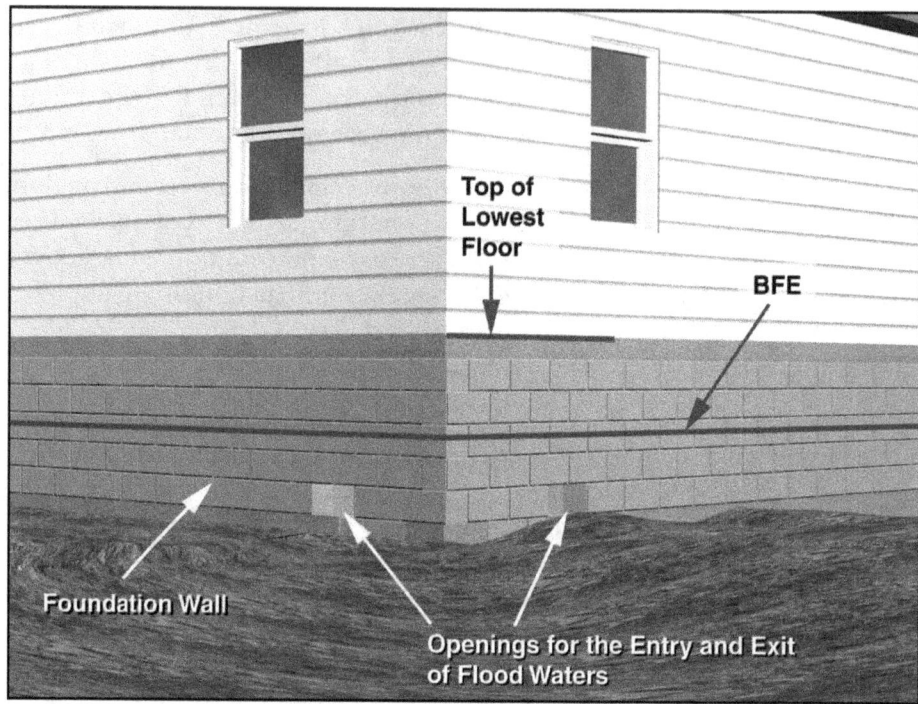

Figure 6

In a new, substantially improved, or substantially damaged building in an A zone, the elevation of the lowest floor must be at or above the BFE.

It is important to note that each of the elevation techniques described and illustrated in this publication depends on the use of continuous walls below the BFE. Therefore, under the NFIP regulations, these techniques may be used only for buildings in A zones, such as the eight case study buildings presented in Chapter 4.

Technical and Regulatory Guidance from FEMA

In the aftermath of Hurricane Andrew, homeowners wanted to begin repairing their damaged houses as soon as possible. They needed immediate guidance concerning repair methods and the floodplain management requirements enforced by Miami-Dade County as a participant in the NFIP. To respond to these needs under the catastrophic conditions resulting from Hurricane Andrew, FEMA, in partnership with other Federal agencies, the State of Florida, and Miami-Dade County, established a Reconstruction Information Center (RIC) in the area where the greatest damage had occurred.

NOTE

In major disasters, FEMA and the affected state will often open one or more Disaster Recovery Centers (DRCs). At a DRC, homeowners and other interested parties can obtain information about how to reduce future flood losses through hazard mitigation.

The RIC provided homeowners with engineering and architectural advice, guidance regarding floodplain management regulations, and information about financial assistance programs operated by FEMA and other agencies. These services were available to all homeowners but were especially valuable to owners of substantially damaged houses.

At the RIC, owners of substantially damaged houses in SFHAs learned that they had two options for complying with the requirement to elevate the lowest floor to or above the flood level:

1. Demolish the remnants of the house and build a new house on the same site with an elevated lowest floor, or

2. Repair the house and elevate the lowest floor as part of the repair process.

Owners of substantially damaged houses in SFHAs that remained structurally sound usually chose the second option—repairing the house and elevating the lowest floor. Depending on how the houses were constructed, their owners had a choice of up to three techniques for elevating the lowest floor (as illustrated on the following pages):

1. Extend the walls of the house upward and raise the lowest floor (Figure 7).

2. Convert the existing lower area of the house to non-habitable space and build a new second story for living space (Figure 8).

3. Lift the entire house, with the floor slab attached, and build a new foundation to elevate the house (Figure 9).

Chapter 3 presents an overview of the three techniques. Chapter 4 covers the techniques in detail and shows how they were used in the repair of eight substantially damaged houses in south Florida.

House at the time
Hurricane Andrew
struck

Figure 7
Technique 1 –
Extend the walls of
the house upward and
raise the lowest floor.

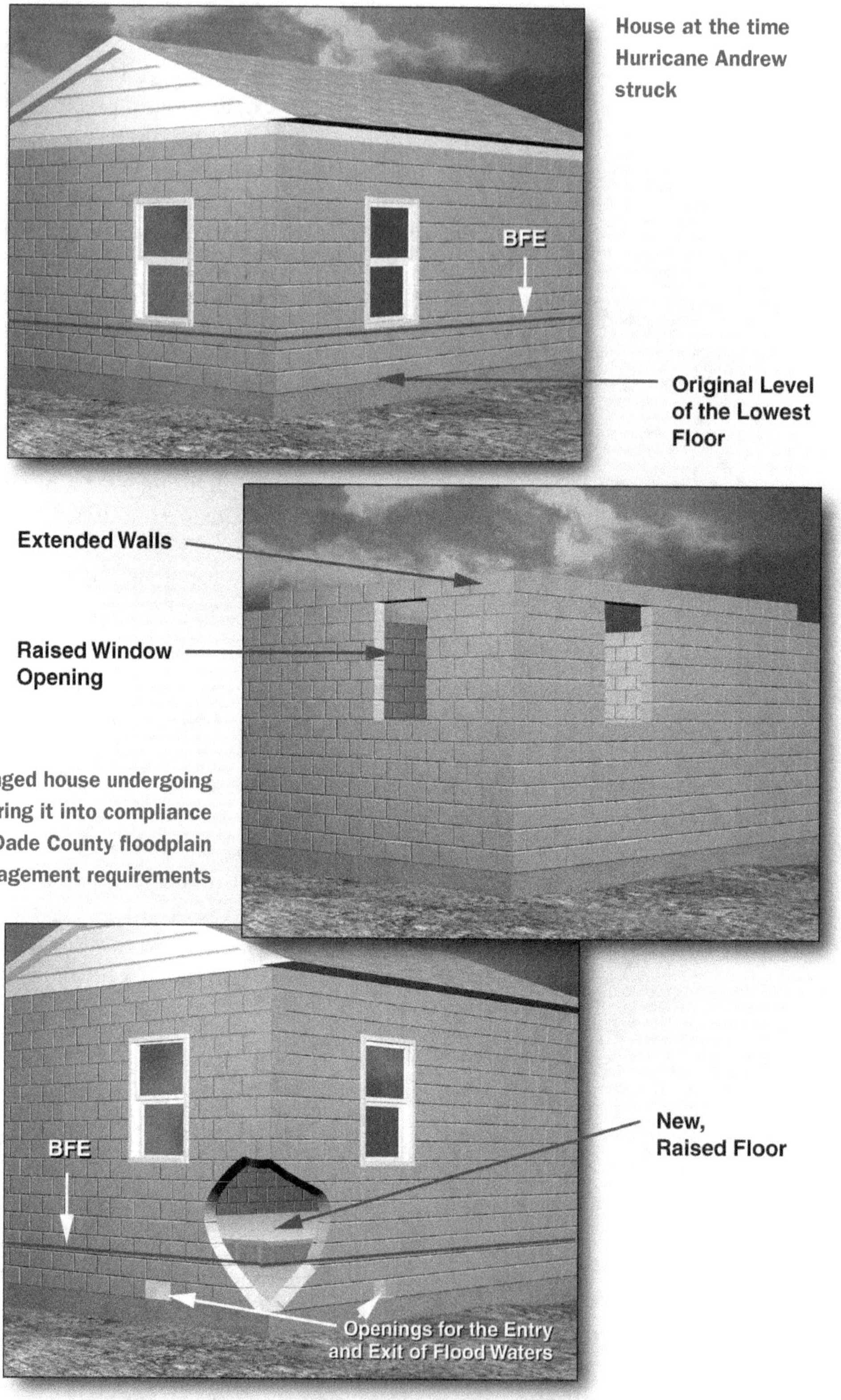

BFE

Original Level
of the Lowest
Floor

Extended Walls

Raised Window
Opening

Substantially damaged house undergoing
repairs that will bring it into compliance
with Miami-Dade County floodplain
management requirements

BFE

New,
Raised Floor

House after
completion of repairs

Openings for the Entry
and Exit of Flood Waters

ABOVE THE FLOOD: ELEVATING YOUR FLOODPRONE HOUSE

Figure 8
Technique 2 –
Convert the existing
lower area of the
house to non-
habitable space and
build a new second
story for living space.

House at the time
Hurricane Andrew
struck

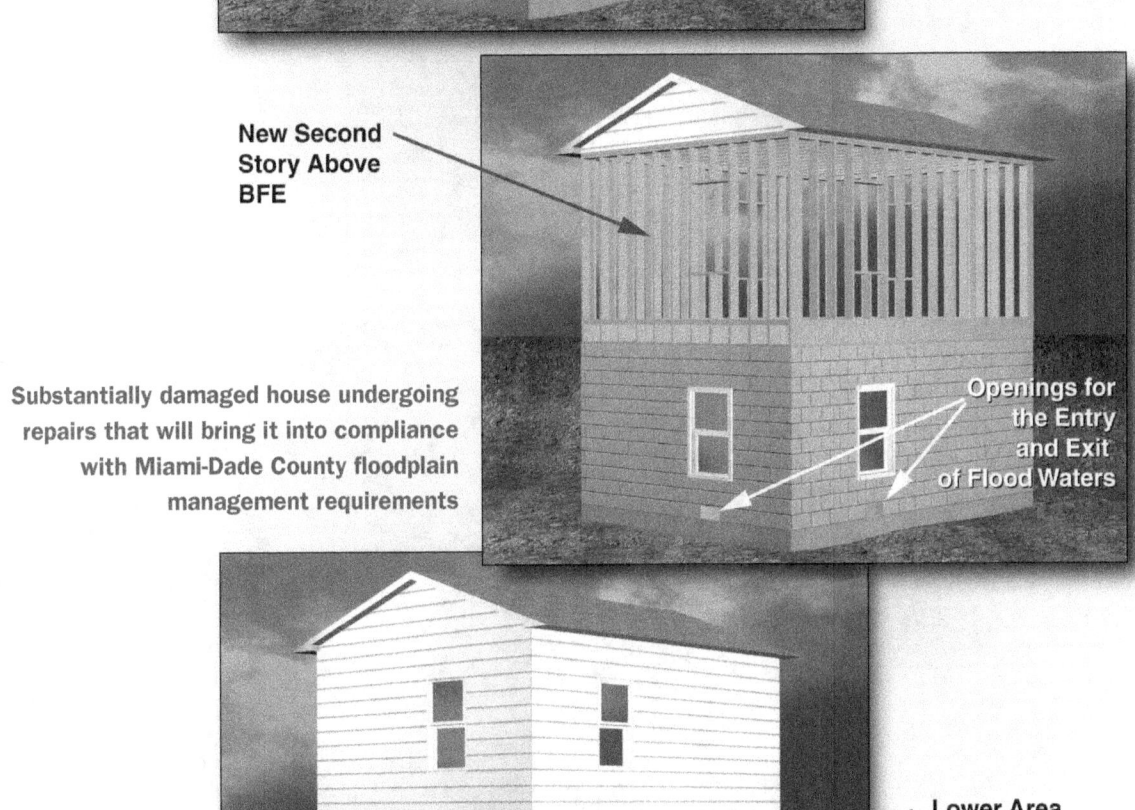

New Second
Story Above
BFE

Substantially damaged house undergoing
repairs that will bring it into compliance
with Miami-Dade County floodplain
management requirements

Openings for
the Entry
and Exit
of Flood Waters

House after
completion of repairs

Lower Area
Converted to
Non-Habitable
Space for
Storage,
Parking, or
Building
Access

Figure 9
Technique 3 –
Lift the entire house,
with the floor slab
attached, and build
a new foundation to
elevate the house.

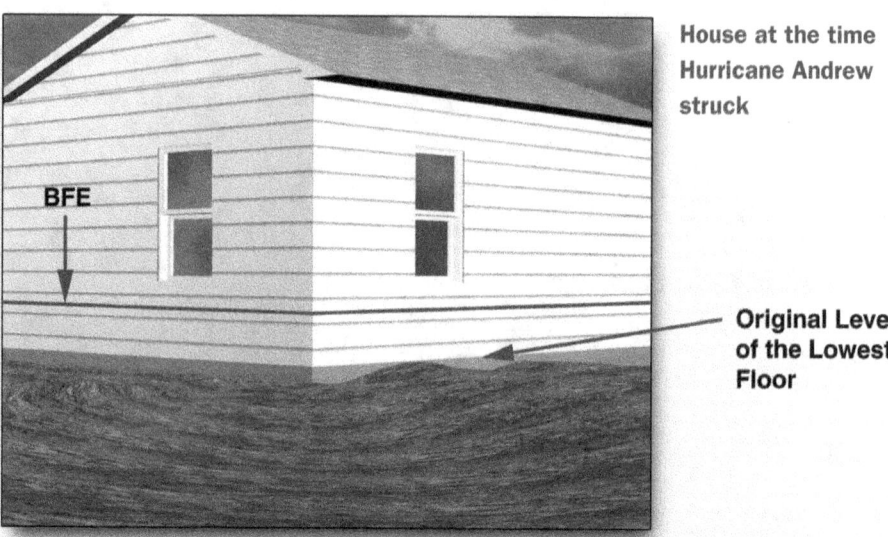

House at the time
Hurricane Andrew
struck

BFE

Original Level
of the Lowest
Floor

Substantially
damaged house
undergoing repairs
that will bring it
into compliance
with Miami-Dade
County floodplain
management
requirements

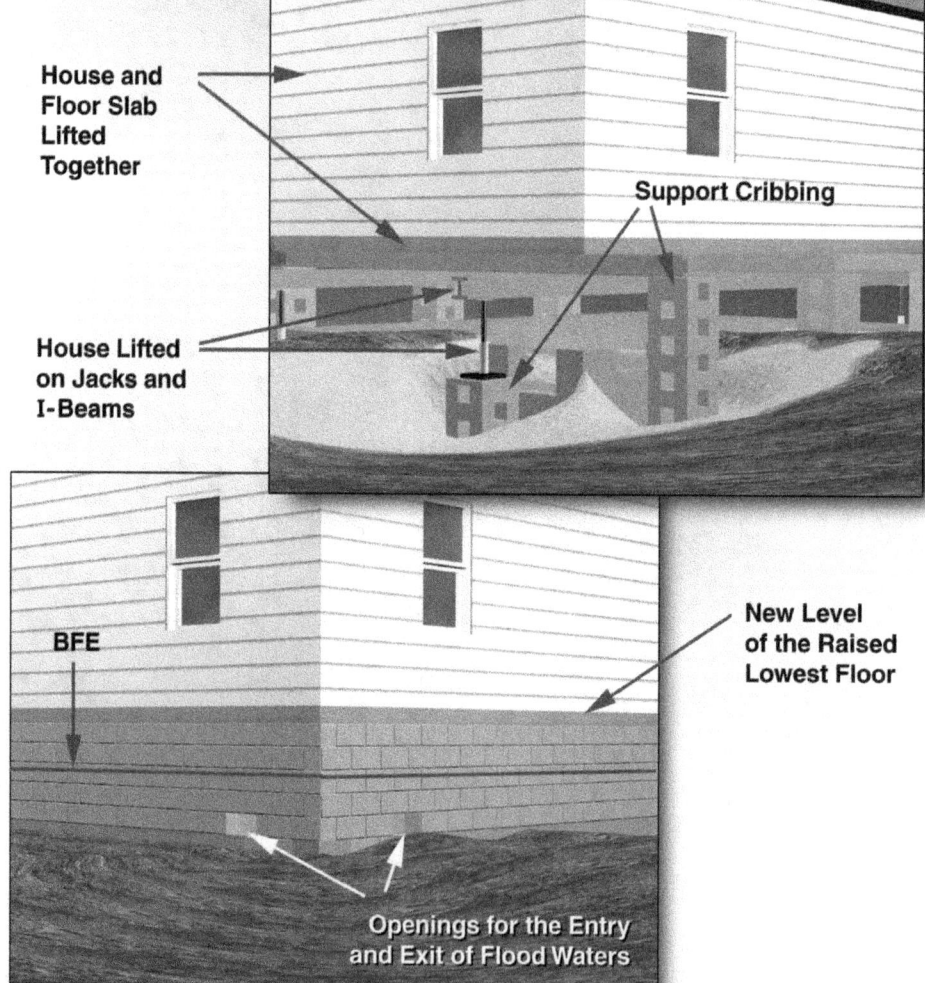

House and
Floor Slab
Lifted
Together

Support Cribbing

House Lifted
on Jacks and
I-Beams

BFE

New Level
of the Raised
Lowest Floor

House after
completion of
repairs

Openings for the Entry
and Exit of Flood Waters

Overview of the Elevation Techniques

Homeowners had a choice of three techniques for elevating their substantially damaged houses.

Technique 1– Extend the Walls of the House Upward and Raise the Lowest Floor

Technique 1 is appropriate for houses with concrete or masonry walls, but not for houses with other types of walls, such as those framed with wood studs, which would be more vulnerable to flood damage. This technique is usually appropriate when the depth of the base flood at the house is no more than 4 or 5 feet above grade. The elevation process begins with the temporary removal of the roof and roof framing, in a single piece if possible (Figure 10). This is commonly done with a crane. The roof is then stored on site so that it can be reinstalled later. The next step is to remove the windows and doors.

Figure 10
The first step in Technique 1 is removing the roof.

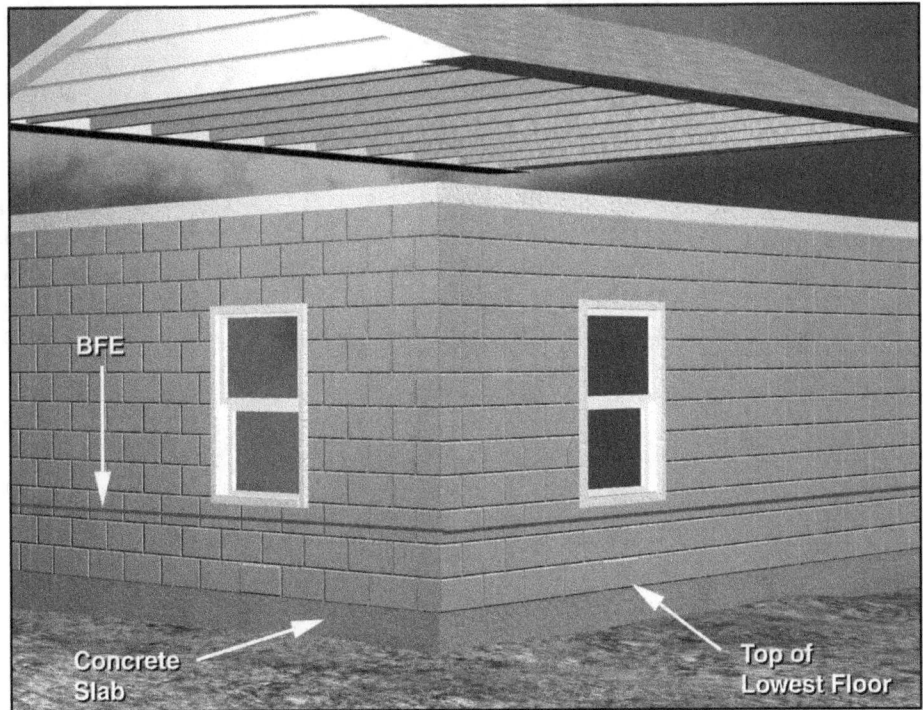

BFE

Concrete Slab

Top of Lowest Floor

After the roof, windows, and doors are removed, several courses of concrete block are added to the tops of the existing walls and to the bottoms of the window openings (Figure 11). A corresponding number of blocks are removed from the tops of the window openings so that the size of the windows will remain the same. In addition, although not shown in Figure 11, concrete bond beams are formed in place at the tops of the extended walls to provide structural reinforcement.

Figure 11
The tops of the walls and bottoms of the window openings are raised with concrete blocks.

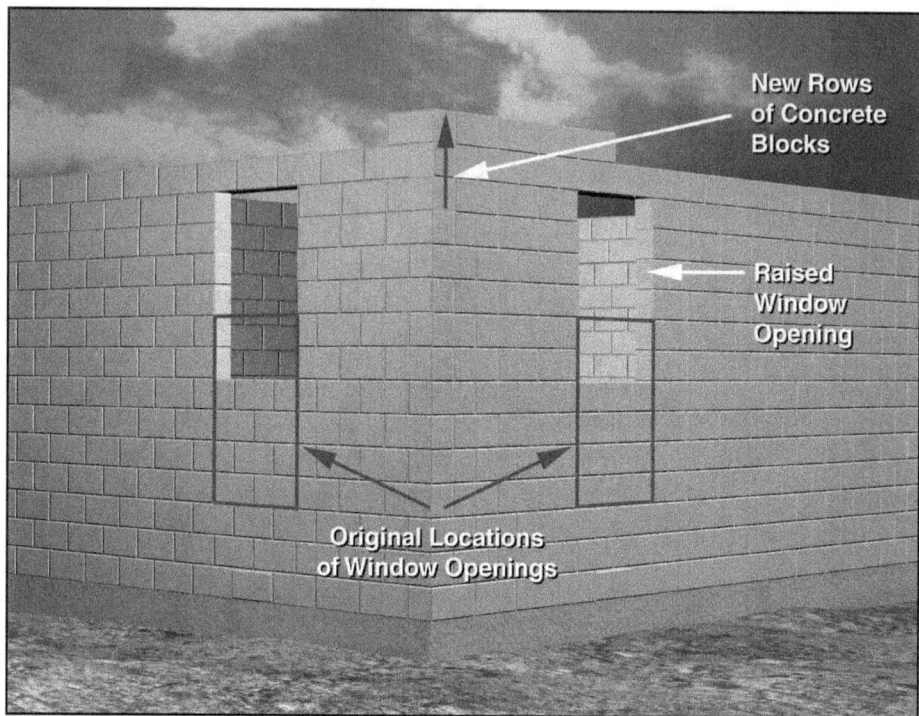

Blocks are removed from the walls of the house at selected locations within 1 foot of the ground (Figure 12). The resulting openings will allow flood waters to flow into and out of the lower area of the house so that the water pressures on both sides of the walls will remain the same. The roof and windows are then replaced, and a new wood-frame floor is constructed above the flood level (Figure 13).

Figure 12
Openings are created in the walls near the ground.

Figure 13
A new wood-frame lowest floor is constructed above the flood level, and the roof, windows, and doors are reinstalled.

A homeowner who chooses Technique 1 may decide to build a new concrete slab floor instead of a wood floor (Figure 14). When this option is chosen, compacted fill dirt or gravel is placed on top of the old slab and the new slab floor is poured on top. Because the area below the new floor is filled with dirt or gravel, wall openings are not required.

Figure 14
An alternative to building an elevated wood-frame floor is installing a new, elevated concrete slab floor on fill placed over the old slab.

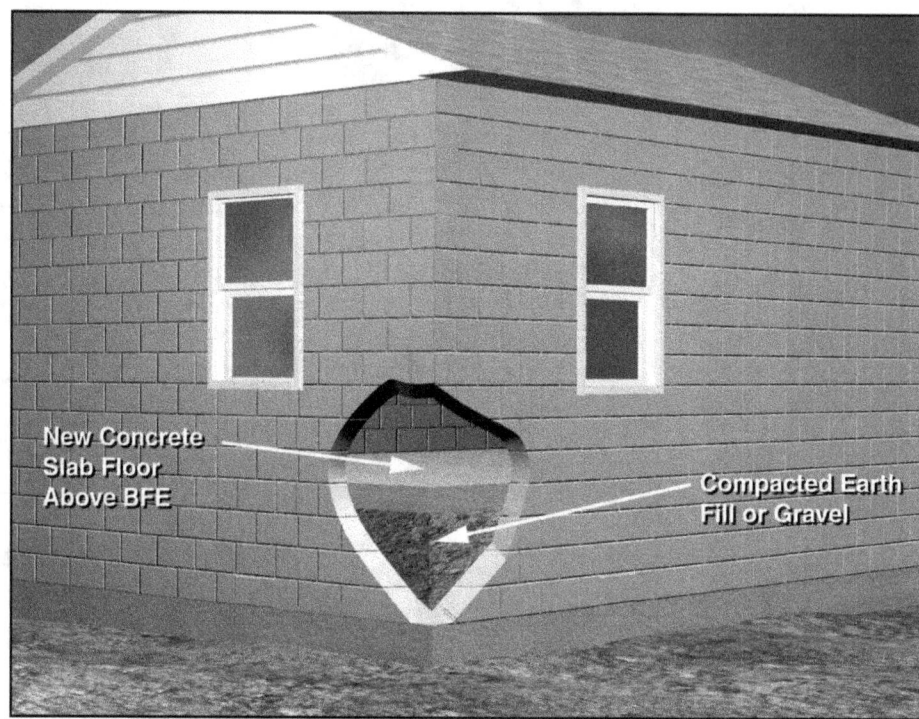

New Concrete Slab Floor Above BFE

Compacted Earth Fill or Gravel

Technique 2 – Convert the Existing Lower Area of the House to Non-Habitable Space and Build a New Second Story for Living Space

When the depth of the base flood at the house is more than 4 or 5 feet above grade, the homeowner will usually find it more practical to add an entire second story to the house. The lower area of the house is then converted to non-habitable space that may be used only for parking, storage, or access to the upper story. Flood waters may still enter this non-habitable lower area. For this reason, Technique 2, like Technique 1, is appropriate for houses with concrete or masonry walls, but not houses with other types of walls.

As in Technique 1, the repairs begin with the temporary removal of the roof and roof framing (Figure 10). After the roof is removed, construction of the new second story begins. First, a new wood-frame floor is built on top of the existing lower-story walls. The second-story walls are framed with metal or wood studs and set in place on the floor (Figure 15).

Figure 15
The new second-story floor and walls are built on top of the existing lower story.

Some homeowners prefer that the second story be constructed of masonry, but wood- or metal-framing is more common, primarily because it is lighter and less expensive. The roof is replaced, and blocks are removed from the walls to allow flood waters to enter and exit. Exterior sheathing is then added to the framed walls of the second story, the new windows are installed, and siding or stucco is applied to the sheathing (Figure 16).

Figure 16
The new second-story walls are covered with siding or stucco.

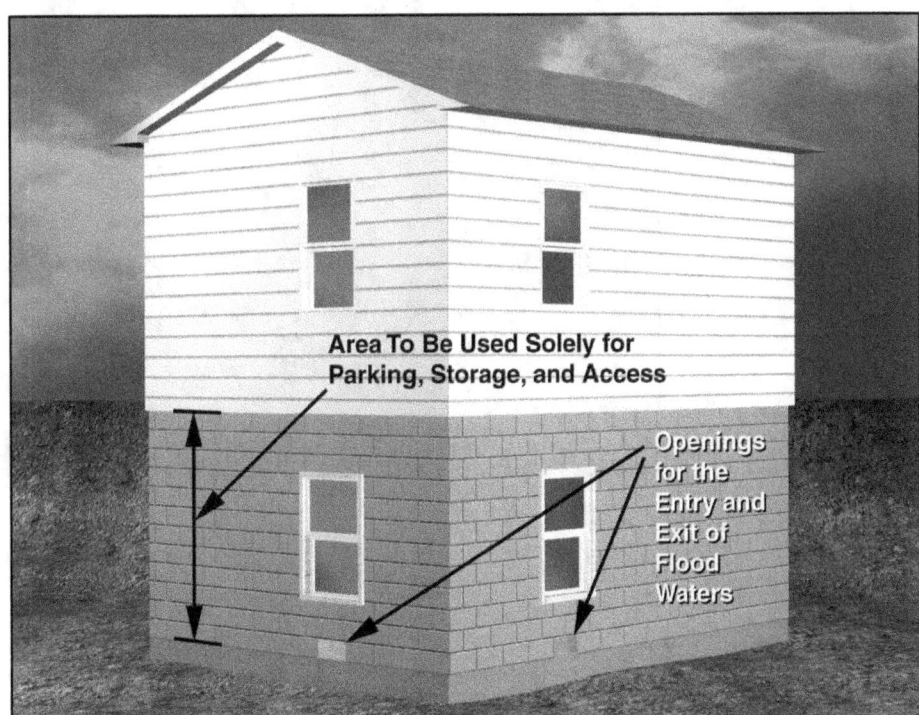

Technique 3 – Lift the Entire House, With the Floor Slab Attached, and Build a New Foundation To Elevate the House.

Technique 3 can be used for houses with wood-frame or masonry walls and is appropriate for a wide range of flood levels. This technique is very different from Techniques 1 and 2. Here, the entire house, including its slab floor, is lifted above the flood level and new masonry foundation walls are built below it. The most common method of lifting the house is to place metal I-beams below the slab and raise the house with jacks.

First, trenches are dug to expose the foundation walls immediately below the slab. Holes are then cut in the foundation walls at intervals around the house, and tunnels are dug under the slab (Figure 17). Jacks are placed in the trenches and large I-beams are inserted through the tunnels and allowed to rest on the jacks. Smaller I-beams are then inserted through the tunnels at right angles to the larger beams and positioned on top of them. The smaller beams support the slab when the house is raised (Figure 18).

Figure 17
Trenches and tunnels under the slab provide access for the jacks and I-beams that will lift the house.

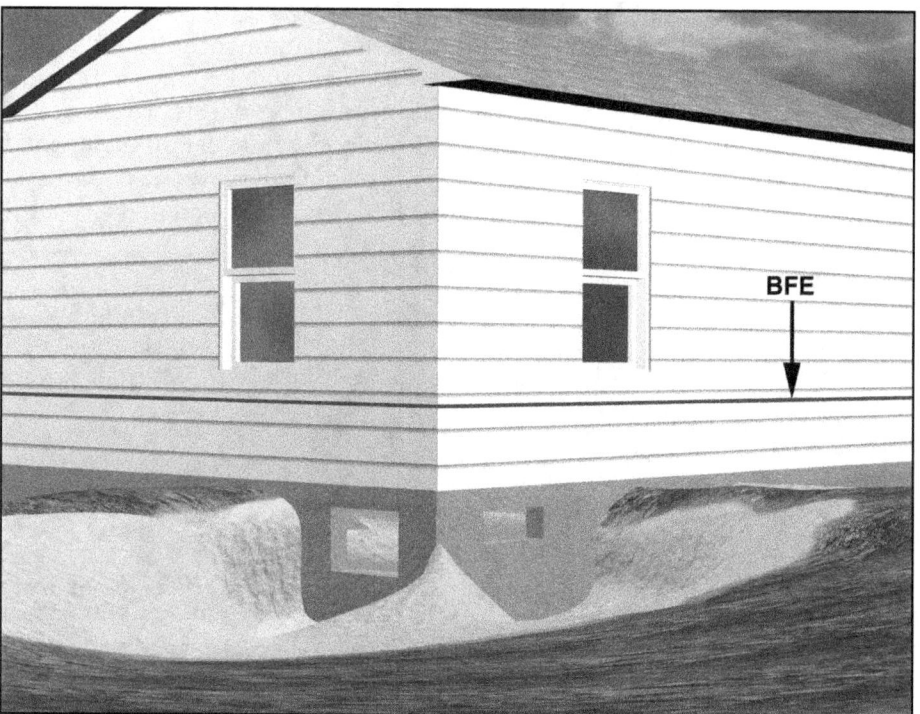

Figure 18
With I-beams and jacks in place, the house is ready to be lifted.

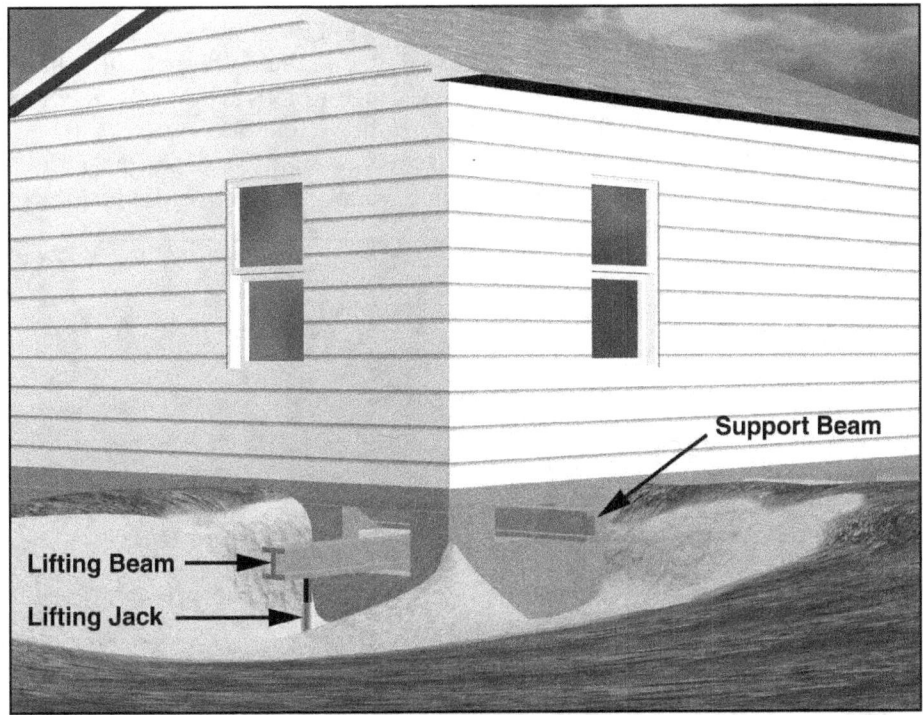

The house is then jacked up. When the jacks have extended as far as possible, the house must be supported temporarily while the jacks are raised. Both the house and the jacks are usually supported on "cribbing"—temporary piles of crisscrossed timbers (Figure 19). The jacks are then used to raise the house higher.

Figure 19
The house is temporarily supported on cribbing.

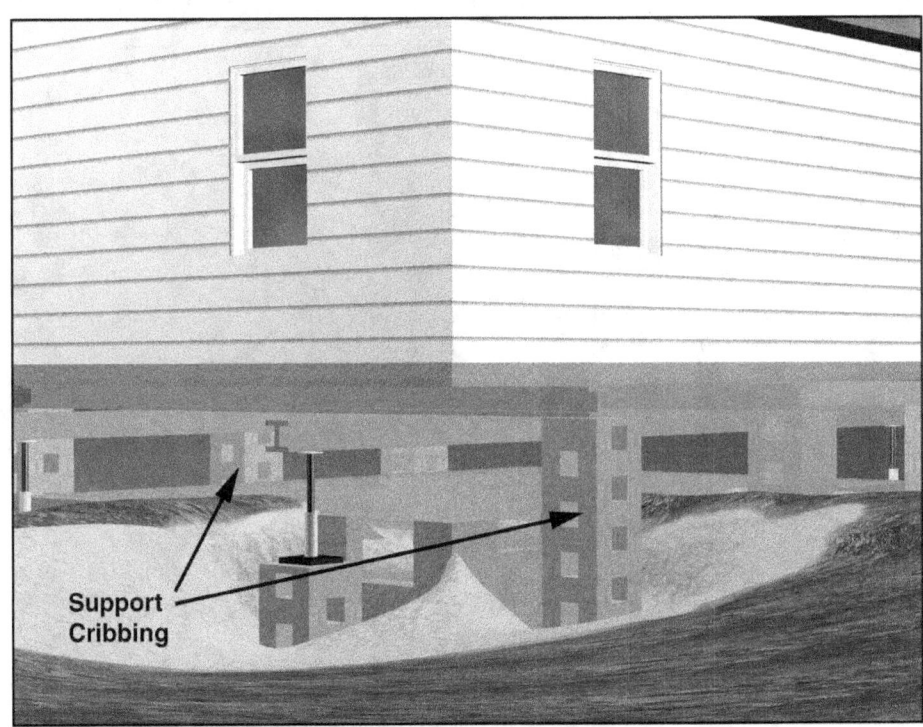

This process is repeated until the house is raised to the desired height. The foundation walls are then extended upward with additional rows of concrete block (Figure 20). As in the previous techniques, openings are made in the walls within 1 foot of the ground so that flood waters will be able to flow into and out of the area below the elevated floor. The jacks and beams are removed, and the openings left around the beams are filled with blocks (Figure 21).

Figure 20
New, extended foundation walls are constructed with concrete blocks.

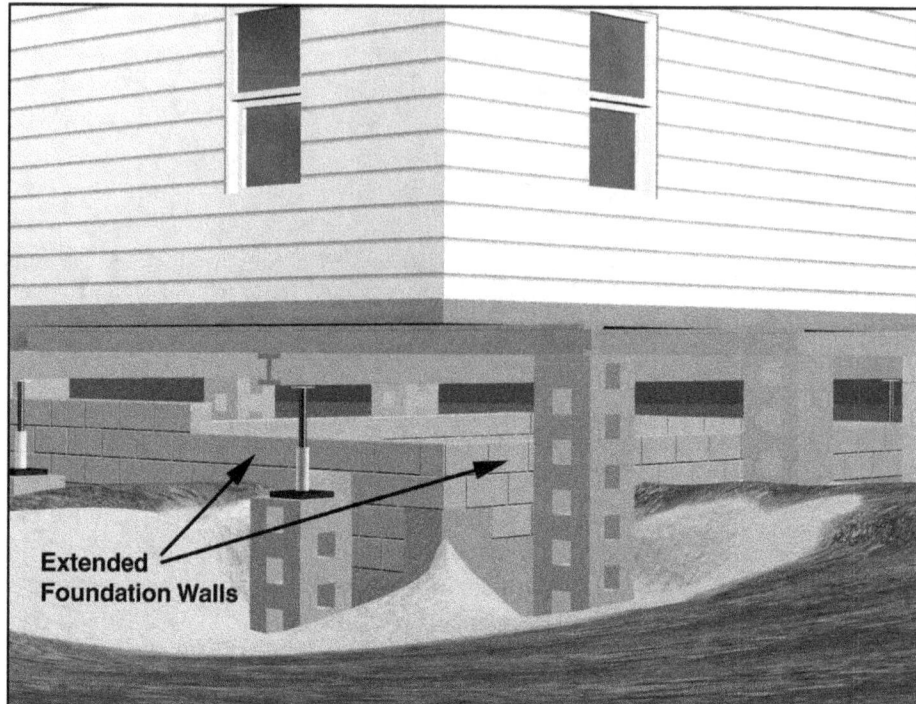

Figure 21
Elevated house and slab on new, extended foundation walls.

Case Studies

Eight case studies demonstrate how substantially damaged houses were elevated in Miami-Dade County After Hurricane Andrew.

The three techniques described in Chapter 3 were used to elevate the eight substantially damaged houses in the following case studies. Three of the houses were elevated with Technique 1, three with Technique 2, one with a combination of Techniques 1 and 2, and one with Technique 3. In each of these houses, the lowest floor was originally below the BFE.

Technique 1 – Extend the Walls of the House Upward and Raise the Lowest Floor.

Case Study 1

The first case study house (Figures 22–32) has masonry walls and a slab-on-grade foundation. The roof of this house was severely damaged by high winds during Hurricane Andrew, and the interior walls suffered extensive damage from flood waters and rain. The owner decided to raise the lowest floor above the BFE by extending the walls upward, placing sand fill on top of the original slab floor, and pouring a new, elevated concrete slab on top.

Figure 22
The front of the house at the beginning of the project. The interior walls and contents, which were destroyed or severely damaged by flood waters, wind, and rain, have been removed. Sand has been placed on top of the old slab to provide the base for the elevated lowest floor. The concrete blocks that will be used to extend the walls can be seen stored in the foreground.

Figure 23

View from the back of the house. The walls have been extended upward with concrete blocks. The plywood visible at the tops of the walls is used to form cast-in-place concrete bond beams that will strengthen the extended walls. The roof trusses shown in the foreground were salvaged for reinstallation. The owner of this house decided to replace the original roof sheathing and shingles with new materials.

Figure 24
Another view of the extended walls. The vertical cuts in the walls next to the windows are for concrete tiedown columns that will be cast in place to further strengthen the extended walls against wind loads. The owner of this house was able to meet the elevation requirement by raising the floor only a few feet, as indicated by the amount that the walls have been extended.

Height of Wall Extension; Floor Will Be Elevated by the Same Amount

Figure 25
This view through the garage door reveals the different levels of the elevated slab floor, in the background, and the unelevated garage floor.

Figure 26
The roof has been rebuilt with the salvaged trusses, and most of the new concrete slab has been poured on top of the sand fill. The open area in the foreground, where plastic sheeting and wire reinforcement can be seen on top of the sand fill, is where the remaining part of the slab will be poured.

Figure 27
As work progresses, the elevated house begins to take shape.

Figure 28
The bottoms of the original window openings are raised with concrete blocks.

Figure 29
Windows and doors are added. The height of the raised front door shows the amount of elevation.

Figure 30
Interior partition walls and utilities are added.

Figure 31
This view from the rear of the house shows that the project is almost complete.

Figure 32
The final product: an attractive elevated house that meets local floodplain management requirements and is now much less vulnerable to flood damage. In addition, the house is now eligible for a lower rate of flood insurance coverage under the NFIP.

Case Study 2

The second house for which Technique 1 was used (Figures 33–38) is similar to the first, and the modifications made are much the same:

- The roof was removed.

- The walls were extended with masonry block.

- Compacted sand fill was placed over the old slab.

- A new slab was poured on top.

- Concrete bond beams and tie columns were installed.

Therefore, this case study focuses on construction details.

Figure 33
Wood framing for a new concrete staircase that will provide access to the elevated floor.

Figure 34
After the new concrete slab is poured, wood framing for interior walls is added.

Figure 35
The electrical system is upgraded to meet current code requirements.

Figure 36
In this view from the front of the house, the amount of elevation is shown by the rows of concrete block on the tops of the original walls and by the raised window openings.

Figure 37
The project nears completion. In this house, as in Case Study 1, the level of the garage floor remains unchanged.

Figure 38
The elevated house is now complete.

Case Study 3

In the third house for which Technique 1 was used (Figures 39–44), the lowest floor was raised only about 1 foot. Otherwise, the work performed was essentially the same, with a few minor exceptions.

Figure 39
The roof of this house was removed as a single piece; the trusses were held together with bracing and portions of the original roof sheathing. This approach made it easier to reinstall the roof at the end of the project.

Figure 40
After the roof was removed and the storm-damaged interior gutted, the walls of the house were extended upward and a new bond beam added at the top.

Figure 41
Note the new bond beam at the top of the extended wall, the new concrete tiedown column at the corner, and the raised window opening.

New Tiedown Column

New Bond Beam

Raised Window Opening

Figure 42
This view from the back of the house shows the height of the elevated slab floor.

Amount by Which Lowest Floor Was Elevated

Figure 43
The owner of this house decided to use light-gauge metal framing for the new interior walls.

Figure 44
The final product. As in the first two houses, the garage floor remains at the original level. The relatively small amount of elevation required for this house has altered its appearance very little.

Technique 2 – Convert the Existing Lower Area of the House to Non-Habitable Space and Build a New Second Story for Living Space.

Case Study 4
The owner of this house (Figures 45–50) chose to build the new second story with reinforced concrete block.

Figure 45
Concrete bond beams similar to those shown earlier were used in this house, but here they were installed on the tops of both the original first-story walls and the new reinforced concrete block second-story walls.

Bond Beam

Figure 46
Concrete tiedown columns, such as the one to the left of the window in this photograph, were also used in this house.

Tiedown
Column

Figure 47
The tiedown columns extend down from the new second-story walls and into the original first-floor walls. The columns tie the first and second stories together and provide a continuous load path that helps the house resist the forces of high winds.

Figure 48
Wood 2 by 4 studs were used to frame the interior walls of the second story.

Figure 49
The house nears completion.

Regulatory Flood Level

Figure 50
Not only does the completed house meet the requirements of local codes and the NFIP regulations, it now includes a substantial amount of parking and storage space below the new living level. In addition, because the lowest floor is now over 4 feet above the regulatory flood elevation, the house is eligible for NFIP flood insurance at a greatly reduced rate of coverage.

Case Study 5
Concrete bond beams and tiedown columns were used in this house (Figures 51–60) as well, but the owner decided to use metal-frame construction rather than concrete block for the new second story.

Figure 51
The storm-damaged first story has been gutted in preparation for construction.

ABOVE THE FLOOD: ELEVATING YOUR FLOODPRONE HOUSE

Figure 52
The existing first-story walls have been strengthened by the addition of concrete block. Metal columns and beams have been added to help support the new second story.

Figure 53
As the second story takes shape, its size in relation to the size of the original house becomes apparent.

Figure 54
Metal framing is used for the new second story, including the walls and roof support system.

Figure 55
Metal framing also supports the floor of the new second story.

Figure 56
One advantage of metal framing is its relatively light weight. An additional advantage is that the screws used to attach metal-frame components provide strong connections.

Figure 57
The project progresses with wiring and other utility work. As in each of the other house elevation projects, all current building code requirements must be met.

Figure 58
The new second story
nears completion.
The roof is made of
formed metal panels.

Figure 59
The exterior
walls consist of
prefabricated
concrete panels.
Innovative techniques
such as those
employed in this
project are helping
homeowners who
need practical and
economical methods
of repairing and
protecting their
houses.

Figure 60
The completed house has the appearance of a typical two-story residence. As in the house in Case Study 2, the lower floor is used only for parking, storage, and building access; the new second story provides the living space.

Case Study 6
The third house for which Technique 2 was used (Figures 61–64) differs from the first two in that the owner decided to build a wood-frame second story.

Figure 61
The wood-frame second story takes shape.

Figure 62
After the wood framing was completed, the roof and exterior wall sheathing were added.

Figure 63
The new second-story walls are securely connected to the original first-floor walls with galvanized metal hurricane straps.

Figure 64
From the outside, the completed house, with its stucco walls, looks like a conventional masonry house.

Combination of Techniques 1 and 2

Case Study 7

Many owners of substantially damaged houses in the areas affected by Hurricane Andrew took advantage of the opportunities afforded by their elevation projects to make additional improvements. For example, the owner of the next house (Figures 65–72) used a combination of Techniques 1 and 2. In addition to extending the walls of the house upward and raising the lowest floor above the BFE, he built a new second-story addition over the garage. The addition was not a necessary part of the elevation process, but it does provide additional living space well above the flood level.

Figure 65

After the house was gutted, the walls were extended upward with reinforced concrete block. In this view from behind the house, the rear wall of the new second story can be seen on the left and the extended first-story wall on the right. Note the new raised window opening in the extended wall, just above the original opening.

Figure 66
The new second-story walls as seen from inside the garage.

Figure 67
The extended first-story walls.

Figure 68
Rather than install a new concrete slab on compacted fill, the owner of this house chose to build a new wood-frame floor above the old concrete slab. This method creates a crawlspace below the new floor.

Bottom of Wood-Framing for Elevated Lowest Floor

Crawlspace

Figure 69
Wood framing is used for the new second story.

Figure 70
Metal hurricane straps are used to tie the structural members together and create a continuous load path from the roof to the foundation.

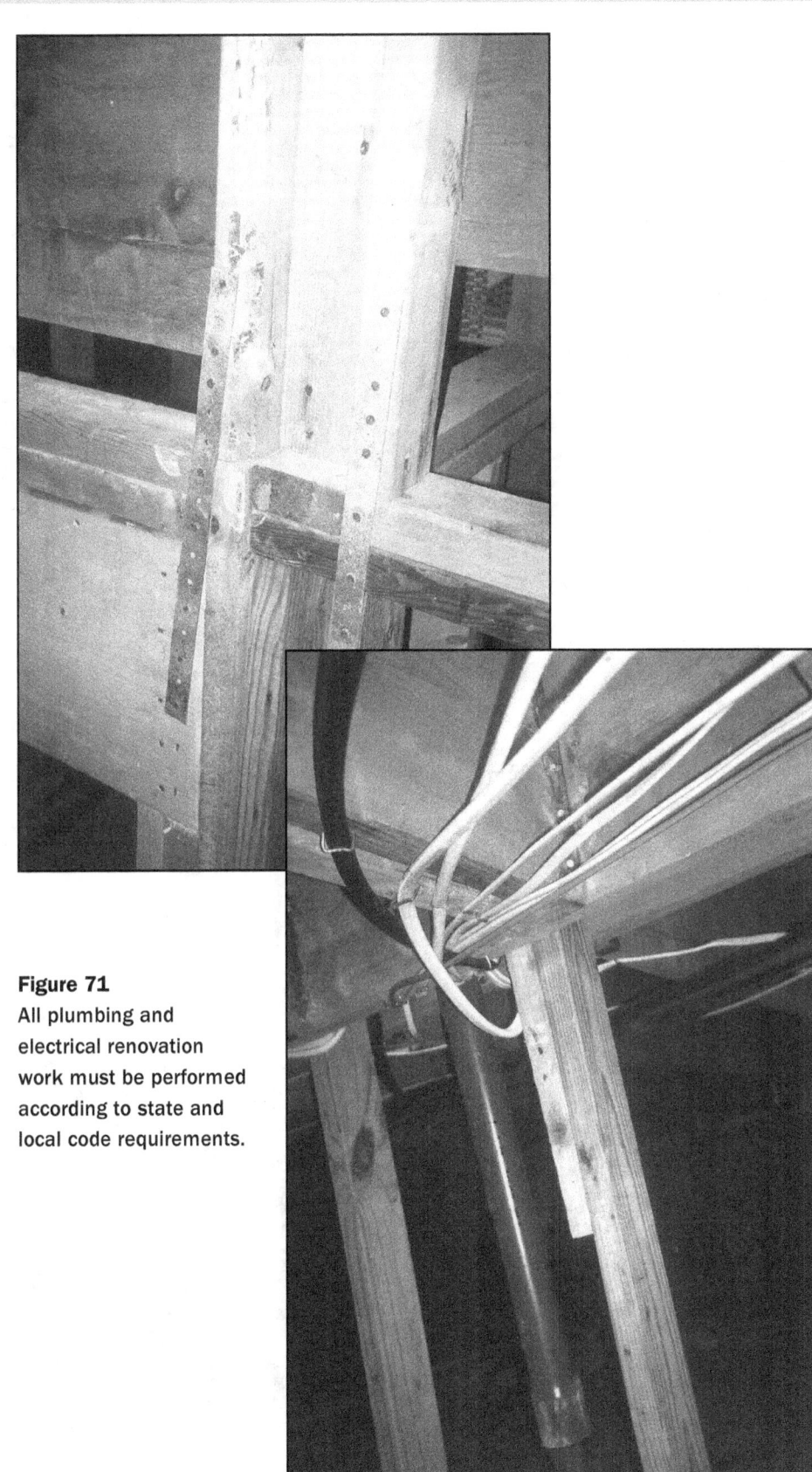

Figure 71
All plumbing and electrical renovation work must be performed according to state and local code requirements.

Figure 72
The completed house is compliant with local floodplain management requirements, is more resistant to flood damage, and provides additional living area above the flood level.

Technique 3 – Lift the Entire House, With the Floor Slab Attached, and Build a New Foundation To Elevate the House.

Case Study 8
Unlike Techniques 1 and 2, which build up from the existing foundation and walls, Technique 3 lifts the entire house with hydraulic jacks and builds a new foundation below it (Figures 73–85).

Figure 73
Like the houses shown previously, this one-story house, with its concrete block walls, concrete slab foundation, and attached garage, is typical of the houses in the area affected by Hurricane Andrew.

Figure 74
In this variation of Technique 3, steel beams are inserted through the walls of the house rather than under the slab. The beams span the length and width of the house and cross one another inside to create a grid. Outside the house, the beams rest on larger beams that will be raised with hydraulic jacks.

Figure 75
Electrical lines and other utilities were disconnected early in the project.

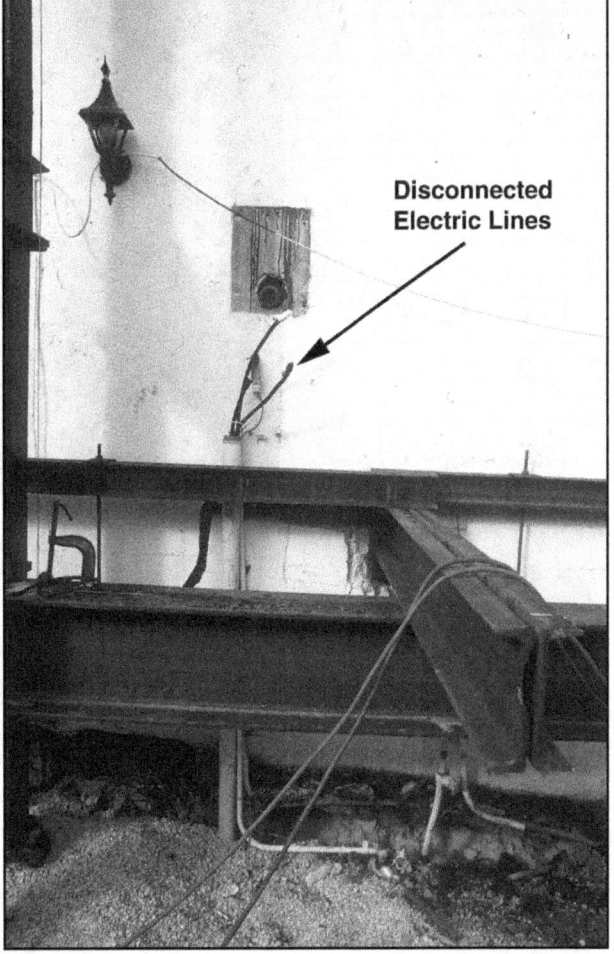

Figure 76
Inside the house, workers drill holes in the concrete slab ...

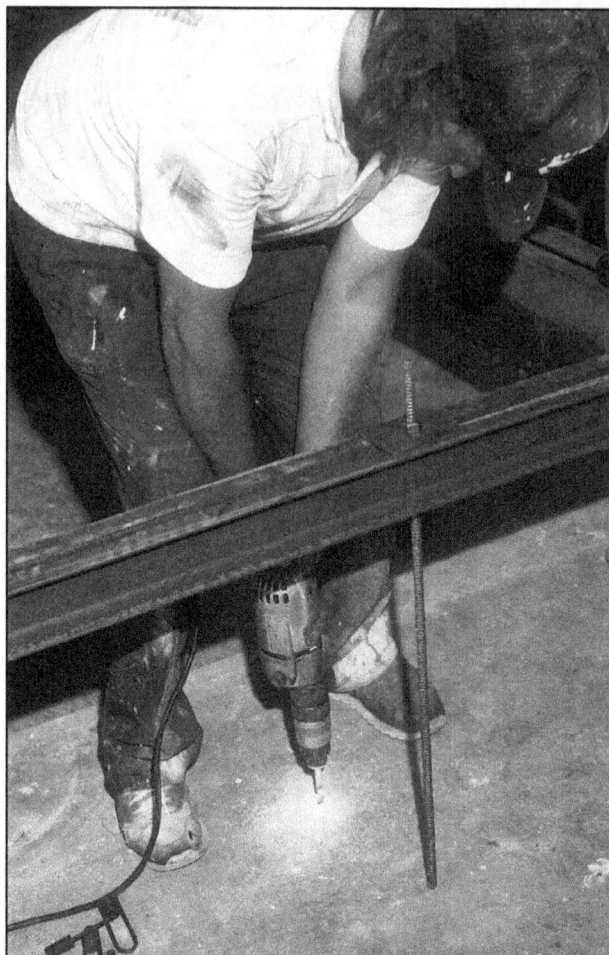

Figure 77
... install anchors ...

Figure 78
... and use hangers to attach the anchors to the grid of steel beams.

Figure 79
The anchors and hangers connect the slab securely to the beams, enabling the beams to raise the slab along with the rest of the house.

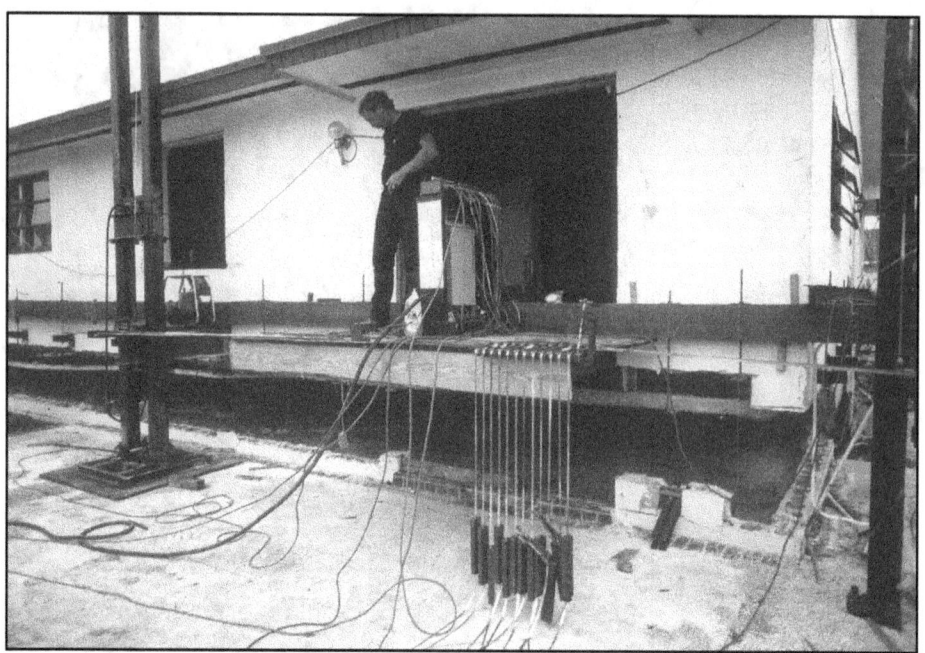

Figure 80
Lifting the house, while simple in theory, is complicated by the need to ensure an equal amount of lift at each jack throughout the process. Too much or too little lift at even one jack can cause the slab and walls to crack. The elevation contractor for this project used a sophisticated jacking system that provided the required level of control.

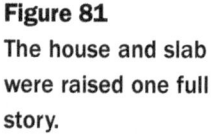

Figure 81
The house and slab were raised one full story.

Figure 82
While the jacks and beams supported the house, new steel foundation members were installed below.

Figure 83
Concrete blocks were brought to the site ...

Figure 84
... and used to build
the lower-level walls.

Figure 85
The completed house,
with lower-level
space for parking and
storage and upper-
level living space,
looks as if it were
originally designed
and built as a two-
story structure.

Summary

The benefits of elevating make it an effective means of protecting a floodprone house.

In communities that participate in the NFIP, new, substantially improved, and substantially damaged houses must be elevated to or above the BFE. As shown by the eight house elevation projects presented in this publication, homeowners may have a choice of three techniques for elevating a slab-on-grade house to comply with local floodplain management requirements and reduce future flood damage.

Elevating provides a number of benefits:

- reduces future flood damage
- can lower flood insurance premium
- can add to the value of the house
- can increase space in the house usable for parking and storage
- can improve the appearance of the house
- helps protect contents
- helps reduce anxiety about future floods

Elevating a substantially damaged house can be expensive, but so can buying or building a comparable replacement house. The cost of elevating will depend of a number of things, including the following:

- size of the house
- type of foundation (e.g., slab-on-grade, crawlspace, basement)
- whether the house has wood-frame, masonry, or concrete walls
- the BFE, which determines the amount of elevation required.

Also, because the costs of labor and construction materials vary across the United States, the location of the house will affect the cost of elevating. However, regardless of these conditions, one of the best times to elevate a floodprone house is when repair or reconstruction is necessary after a flood or other damaging event. The benefits of elevating, coupled with the desire of many homeowners to remain in their neighborhoods, makes elevating an attractive solution to flood problems.

It is important to note that masonry-wall slab-on-grade houses, such as the eight case study houses presented in this publication, are among the most difficult to elevate. In general, masonry, wood-frame, and metal-frame houses on other types of foundations, such as crawlspaces, basements, pilings, piers, or posts, are easier and less expensive to elevate. Therefore, elevating will often be the most practical means of protecting a house from flooding and complying with floodplain management requirements.

Additional Information

Information about protecting floodprone houses is available from FEMA and other sources.

NOTE

To learn more about flood hazards, floodplain management requirements, and building codes in your community, check with your local floodplain administrator, building official, city engineer, or planning and zoning administrator.

NOTE

A number of Federal and non-Federal programs provide financial assistance for retrofitting projects, including house elevation. FEMA's *Homeowner's Guide to Retrofitting* (FEMA 312) lists these programs and describes the types of assistance available.

FEMA has produced many technical guides and manuals that provide additional information about methods of protecting floodprone houses, including elevation techniques. Some of these documents are intended primarily for homeowners and non-technical readers; others are designed specifically to meet the needs of engineers, architects, and building officials.

FEMA Guides and Manuals for Both Non-Technical and Technical Readers

Homeowner's Guide to Retrofitting– Six Ways to Protect Your House From Flooding
FEMA Publication No. 312

This handbook is intended for non-technical readers who would like more information about flood protection methods. Illustrated discussions of house elevation, wet floodproofing, house relocation, dry floodproofing, levees and floodwalls, and demolition are supplemented with cost estimates, checklists, and decision-making worksheets.

NFIP Technical Bulletin Series
TB-1 through TB-9

FEMA's NFIP Technical Bulletins are intended for a broad range of readers, including homeowners, local officials, and design professionals, who need guidance concerning NFIP regulatory requirements that apply to buildings in SFHAs. Topics addressed by the bulletins that may be of interest to readers of this publication include the requirement for openings in foundation walls below the BFE (TB-1), flood-resistant materials requirements (TB-2), wet floodproofing requirements (TB-7), and corrosion protection for metal connectors in coastal areas (TB-8).

Protecting Building Utilities From Flood Damage – Principles and Practices for the Design and Construction of Flood Resistant Building Utility Systems
FEMA Publication No. 348

This manual is intended for developers, architects, engineers, builders, code officials, and homeowners who are involved in designing and constructing building utility systems for residential and non-residential structures. The manual discusses flood-protective design and construction of utility systems for new buildings and modifications to utility systems in existing buildings.

FEMA Guides and Manuals for Engineers, Architects, Building Officials, and Other Technical Readers

Coastal Construction Manual – Principles and Practices of Planning, Siting, Designing, Constructing, and Maintaining Residential Buildings in Coastal Areas

Third Edition
FEMA Publication No. 55

This three-volume manual is intended for architects, engineers, building professionals, and community officials who need technical guidance concerning the proper methods of planning, siting, designing, constructing, and maintaining residential buildings in coastal areas subject to flood, wind, and seismic hazards. The manual includes a summary of past coastal hazard events, such as hurricanes, northeasters, and tsunamis; a discussion of coastal hazards and regulatory requirements that affect coastal construction; and detailed design guidance, including formulas and example problems.

Engineering Principles and Practices for Retrofitting Flood Prone Residential Buildings

FEMA Publication No. 259

This manual is intended for architects, engineers, and building professionals who need technical guidance concerning flood protection techniques that can be applied to existing buildings. Detailed specifications, computation examples, and cost data are presented.

In addition, this publication on house elevation in south Florida is available on both CD-ROM and videotape. To order copies of FEMA publications, including videos and CD-ROMs, call the FEMA Publications Distribution Facility at 1-800-480-2520.

For more information about hazard mitigation and other subjects in emergency management, visit FEMA's web site:

www.fema.gov